INTRODUCTION

The ability to sight-read fluently is an essential part of your training as a cellist, whether you intend to play professionally, or simply for enjoyment. Yet the *study* of sight-reading is often badly neglected by young players and is frequently regarded as no more than an unpleasant side-line. If you become a good sight-reader you will be able to learn pieces more quickly, play in ensembles and orchestras with confidence and of course earn extra marks in grade exams!

Using the workbook

The purpose of this workbook is to incorporate sight-reading regularly into your practice and lessons, and to help you prepare for the sight-reading test in grade examinations. It offers you a progressive series of enjoyable and stimulating stages in which, with careful work, you should show considerable improvement from week to week.

Each stage consists of two parts: firstly, exercises which you should prepare in advance, along with a short piece with questions; and secondly, a set of unprepared tests.

Your teacher will mark your work according to accuracy. Each stage carries a maximum of 50 marks as follows:

    2 marks for each of the six questions relating to the prepared piece (total 12).
    18 marks for the piece itself.
    20 marks for the unprepared test. (Teachers should devise a similar series of questions for the unprepared test and take the answers into account when allocating a final mark.)

Space is given at each stage for you to keep a running total of your marks as you progress. If you are scoring 40 or more each time you are doing well!

There are five different types of exercise:

1 **Rhythmic exercises** It is very important that you should be able to feel and maintain a steady beat. These exercises will help develop this ability. There are at least four ways of doing them: clap or tap the lower line (the beat or pulse) while singing the upper line to 'la'; tap the lower line with your foot and clap the upper line; on a table or flat surface, tap the lower line with one hand and the upper line with the other; 'play' the lower line on a metronome and clap or tap the upper line.

2 **Sight-singing exercises** Being able to hear music accurately in your head is a wonderful skill all musicians should develop. It will promote both accuracy and fluency and help develop secure intonation. First you should try to hear the exercises in your head and then sing them out loud at a comfortable pitch level.

3 **Melodic exercises** Fluent sight-reading depends on recognising melodic shapes at a glance. These shapes are often related to scales and arpeggios. Study these exercises carefully; they contain many melodic shapes that you will encounter time and time again. Try hearing them through in your head first, then sing them out loud at a comfortable octave for your voice. Then play them.

4 **A prepared piece with questions** You should prepare carefully both the piece and the questions, which are to help you think about and understand the music before you play it.

5 **Unprepared exercises** Finally you should work through the *unprepared* tests which should be read at *sight*.

Remember to feel the beat throughout each piece and to keep going at a steady and even tempo. Always try to look ahead, at least to the next note or beat.

The author wishes to thank Charles Ellis for many valuable suggestions.

NAME

EXAMINATION RECORD

Grade	Date	Mark

TEACHER'S NAME

TELEPHONE

© 1998 by Faber Music Ltd
First published in 1998 by Faber Music Ltd
3 Queen Square London WC1N 3AU
Music and text set by Wessex Music Services
Cover illustration by Drew Hillier
Printed in England by Caligraving Ltd
All rights reserved

ISBN 0-571-51873-7

STAGE 1

♩ ⅃ **2/4** ⊓ **Down bow**
          ∨ **Up bow**

RHYTHMIC EXERCISES

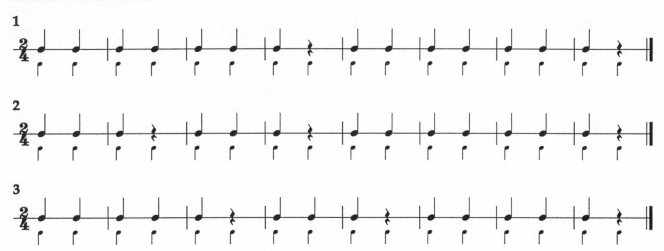

SIGHT-SINGING   Always sing the sight-singing exercises at your own pitch. Try to 'pre-hear' each note before you sing it.

MELODIC EXERCISES   Try to hear each exercise in your head first, then sing it out loud at a comfortable pitch in your own vocal range, then play it.

4

PREPARED PIECE

1 In which key is this piece?

2 What does *Moderato* mean?

3 Which of the following words do you think best describe this piece?
   sad, comical, angry, lazy, energetic.

4 What does f *(forte)* mean?

5 How many beats are there in each bar?

6 Clap the first four bars. Now try clapping them from memory.

Marks*

Total:

Moderato

9

Mark:

Prepared work total:

Unprepared:

Total:

* The mark boxes are to be filled in by your teacher.

UNPREPARED TESTS

1

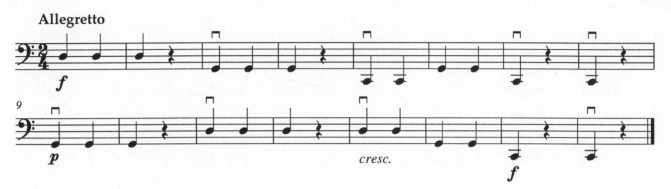

2

3

STAGE 2

$\frac{4}{4}$ ♩

Sharps (#)

RHYTHMIC EXERCISES

1

2

3

SIGHT-SINGING

1

2

MELODIC EXERCISES

1

2

3

4

PREPARED PIECE

1 How many beats are there in each bar? □

2 What are the letter names of all the notes in the first line? □

3 How many beats is each crotchet (♩) and each minim (𝅗𝅥) worth? □

4 How many beats is each crotchet rest (𝄽) worth? □

5 What does *Andante* mean? □

6 What does *f (forte)* indicate? □

Total: □

Mark: □

Prepared work total: □

Unprepared: □

Total: □

Running totals:

1	2

UNPREPARED TESTS

1

Andante

2

Allegretto

3

Moderato

STAGE 3

 G major

---

RHYTHMIC EXERCISES

1

2

3

SIGHT-SINGING

1   **2**

MELODIC EXERCISES   Remember the key-signature – at the beginning of each new line remind yourself of the key.
Play the scale and arpeggio of G major before you begin the following exercises.

1

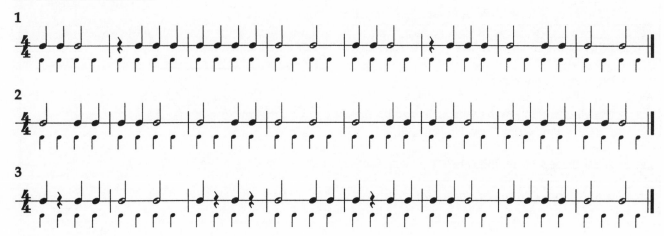

2

'Feel' a strong first beat in the next exercise.

3

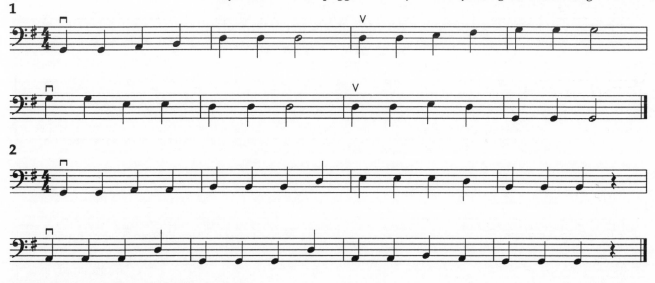

PREPARED PIECE

1 What does $\frac{4}{4}$ indicate? How many beats will you count in each bar?

2 Where does the pattern in bars 8-10 reoccur?

3 What key is the piece in?

4 Which of the following words do you think best describe this piece?
   happy, serious, fast, bouncy, dull

5 What does $\boldsymbol{f}$ *(forte)* indicate?

6 What is the meaning of *Allegretto?*

Total: ☐

Allegretto

Mark: ☐

Prepared work total: ☐

Unprepared: ☐

Total: ☐

Running totals:

1	2	3

UNPREPARED TESTS

STAGE 4

RHYTHMIC EXERCISES

1

2

3

SIGHT-SINGING

1

2

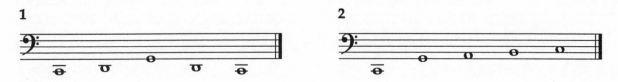

MELODIC EXERCISES   Play the scale and arpeggio of C major before you begin the following exercises.

1

2

3

4

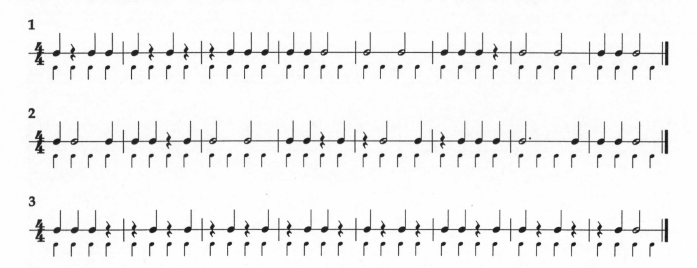

PREPARED PIECE

1 In which key is this piece?

2 What does *rit.* mean?

3 What is the effect of the curved line joining two notes (eg. bar 1)? What is it called?

4 What does *p (piano)* mean?

5 What does the marking in bar 8 mean?

6 Clap the last four bars. Now try clapping them from memory.

Total:

Andante

Mark:

Prepared work total:

Unprepared:

Total:

Running totals:

1	2	3	4

14

UNPREPARED TESTS

1

Allegretto

STAGE 5

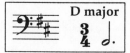

RHYTHMIC EXERCISES

SIGHT-SINGING

MELODIC EXERCISES

Play the scale and arpeggio of D major before you begin the following exercises.

PREPARED PIECE

1 What does **¾** mean? ☐

2 Mark the F sharps and C sharps with a cross. ☐

3 How many beats is each dotted minim (𝅗𝅥.) worth? ☐

4 What is the letter name of the third note in bar 3? ☐

5 What does *mf (mezzo-forte)* indicate? ☐

6 What does **Rall.** mean? ☐

Total: ☐

Mark: ☐

Prepared work total: ☐

Unprepared: ☐

Total: ☐

Running totals:

1	2	3	4	5

UNPREPARED TESTS

1

Allegretto

2

Andante con moto

3

Moderato, tempo di valse

STAGE 6

The minim rest

RHYTHMIC EXERCISES

SIGHT-SINGING

MELODIC EXERCISES

PREPARED PIECE

1 How many beats is each 𝅗𝅥 and each 𝅗𝅥. worth?

2 Which of the following words do you think best describes this piece?
  flowing, heavy, happy, gentle, busy

3 How many beats rest is ▬ worth?

4 What does **p** *(piano)* indicate?

5 How will you achieve the effect of the long *crescendo* in bars 11-14?

6 What is the meaning of *Moderato?*

Total:

Moderato

Mark:

Prepared work total:

Unprepared:

Total:

Running totals:

1	2	3	4	5	6

UNPREPARED TESTS

STAGE 7

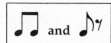

RHYTHMIC EXERCISES

1

2

3

4

SIGHT-SINGING

1

2

3

MELODIC EXERCISES

1

2

3

4

PREPARED PIECE

1 What does **4/4** indicate?

2 Clap the rhythm of the last four bars. Now try clapping them from memory.

3 How many dynamics levels are there?

4 What are the letter names of the notes in the last line?

5 What does ⟍ indicate?

6 What is the meaning of *Allegro moderato?*

Total:

Allegro moderato

Mark:

Prepared work total:

Unprepared:

Total:

Running totals:

1	2	3	4	5	6	7

UNPREPARED TESTS

STAGE 8

A major

RHYTHMIC EXERCISES

SIGHT-SINGING

MELODIC EXERCISES

Play the scale and arpeggio of A major before you begin the following exercises.

PREPARED PIECE

1 How many beats are there in each bar?

2 In which key is this piece?

3 Mark the G sharps with a cross.

4 What does the mark ＞ in bar 3 mean?

5 Clap this rhythm:

6 What does *Andante grazioso* mean? How will you achieve the effect?

Total:

Andante grazioso

Mark:

Prepared work total:

Unprepared:

Total:

Running totals:

1	2	3	4	5	6	7	8

UNPREPARED TESTS

1

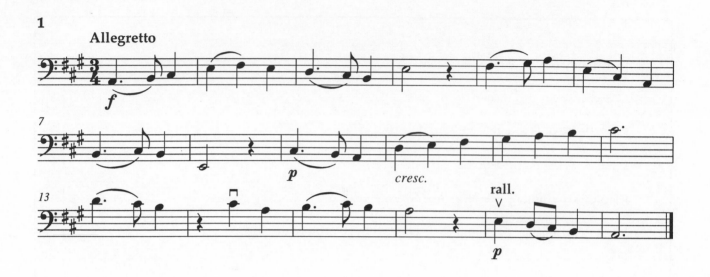

2

3

STAGE 9

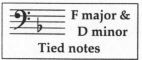

F major &
D minor
Tied notes

RHYTHMIC EXERCISES

1

2

3

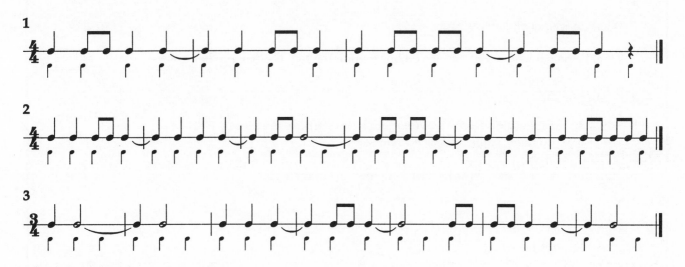

SIGHT-SINGING

1
2

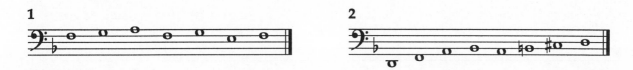

MELODIC EXERCISES   Play the scale and arpeggio of F major before you begin the following exercises.

1

2

Play the scale and arpeggio of D minor before you begin the following exercises.

3

4

PREPARED PIECE

1 In which key is this piece?

2 What does *Andantino* mean?

3 What is the name given to the curved line joining the two F's (bar 1 to bar 2)?

4 What does **mp** *(mezzo-piano)* mean?

5 Which of the following words do you think best describes the piece?
    funny, strong, sleepy, delicate, solemn

6 Clap the last four bars. Now try clapping them from memory.

Total:

Mark:

Prepared work total:

Unprepared:

Total:

Running totals:

1	2	3	4	5	6	7	8	9

UNPREPARED TESTS

1

Grazioso

2

Allegretto

3

Marziale

STAGE 10

RHYTHMIC EXERCISES

1

2

3

SIGHT-SINGING

1   **2**

MELODIC EXERCISES

1

Play the scale and arpeggio of B♭ major before you begin the following exercises.

2

3

4

PREPARED PIECE

1 In which key is this piece? ☐

2 What does *Allegro giocoso* mean? ☐

3 How would you describe the character of this piece? ☐

4 Which is the softest part of the piece? ☐

5 Where does the rhythm of the first two bars re-appear? ☐

6 Clap the last two bars. Now try clapping them from memory. ☐

Total: ☐

Allegro giocoso

Mark: ☐

Prepared work total: ☐

Unprepared: ☐

Total: ☐

Running totals:

1	2	3	4	5	6	7	8	9	10

UNPREPARED TESTS

1

2

3

STAGE 11

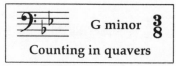

G minor

Counting in quavers

RHYTHMIC EXERCISES

1

2

3

SIGHT-SINGING

1

2

MELODIC EXERCISES

Play the scale and arpeggio of G minor before you begin the following exercises.

1

2

3

4

5

34

PREPARED PIECE

1 In which key is this piece?

2 What will you count?

3 How would you describe the character of this piece?

4 What does *poco rall.* mean?

5 Where does the rhythm of the first four bars re-appear?

6 Look at the first four bars for a few moments. Now try playing them from memory.

Total:

Mark:

Prepared work total:

Unprepared:

Total:

Running totals:

1	2	3	4	5	6	7	8	9	10	11

UNPREPARED TESTS

1

Andantino

2

Giocoso

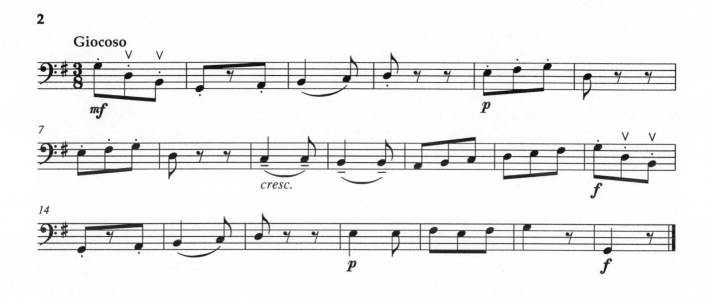

3

Con moto

A SIGHT-READING CHECKLIST

Before you play a piece at sight always remember to consider the following:

1   Look at the key-signature, and find the notes which need raising or lowering.
2   Look at the time-signature and decide how you will count the piece.
3   Notice any accidentals occurring during the piece.
4   Notice scale and arpeggio patterns.
5   Notice melodic or rhythmic patterns that recur.
6   Work out leger-line notes if necessary.
7   Notice dynamic and other markings.
8   Look at the tempo mark, any technical difficulties and, taking both into account, decide what speed to play.
9   Count at least one bar in (in your head) before you begin, to establish the pulse.
10   Decide what the character of the music is and how you will achieve this.

When performing your sight-reading piece, always remember to:

1   CONTINUE TO COUNT THROUGHOUT THE PIECE.
2   Keep going at a steady and even tempo.
3   Ignore mistakes.
4   Check the key-signature at the beginning of each line.
5   Look ahead – at least to the next note or beat.
6   Play expressively and try to give character to your performance; in other words play *musically*.

SKIMMING

In most examinations you will be given a short period of time to study your piece before you have to play it. If you learn to skim-read, you will be able to pick up an enormous amount of information in a very short time. Read through the music fairly quickly, making sure you take in the whole piece. Do this for about 30 seconds and then, removing the music, get your teacher or a friend to ask you questions (based on the headings above). Try it again in 20 seconds, then 10 (or even less!) In time you will be able to develop this very useful ability.

GRADING

The following is an approximate guide to grade levels. Students are encouraged to go beyond their particular grade levels to promote confidence!

Stage 1 - 4   Grade 1
Stage 4 - 8   Grade 2
Stage 8 - 11   Grade 3